HOW TO SAY NO WITHOUT SAYING

NO

Eleanor "C-PASS" Jones

HOW TO SAY NO WITHOUT SAYING NO

Eleanor "C-PASS" Jones

KP PUBLISHING

Los Angeles

Copyright 2021 by Eleanor "C-PASS" Jones

All rights reserved. In accordance with the U.S. Copyright Act of 1976, the scanning, uploading, and electronic sharing of any part of this book without the permission of the publisher is unlawful piracy and theft of the author's intellectual property. If you would like to use material from this book (other than for review purposes), prior written permission must be obtained by contacting the publisher at info@knowledgepowerinc.com.

Thank you for your support of the author's rights.
ISBN: 978-1-950936-78-6   (Hardcover)
ISBN: 978-1-950936-79-3   (Ebook)
Library of Congress Control Number:

Editor: KP Publishing Services
Cover/BookDesign: Juan Roberts for Creative Lunacy
Literary Director: Sandra Slayton James

Published by:
KP PUBLISHING COMPANY
Publisher of Fiction, Nonfiction & Children's Books
Valencia, CA 91355
www.kp-pub.com

Printed in the United States of America

CONTENTS

Chapter One — 1
OVERVIEW

Chapter Two — 7
IF

Chapter Three — 13
AS SOON AS

Chapter Four — 17
WHEN

Chapter Five — 21
BUT

Chapter Six — 25
AUTHOR'S PERSPECTIVE AND EXPERIEINCES

Chapter Seven — 33
RESPONSES YOU'VE USED

Chapter Eight — 37
RESPONSES YOU'VE RECEIVED

A Little Help from My Friends — 40

CHAPTER ONE

OVERVIEW

OVERVIEW

Some people have no problem saying "No" unequivocally. On the other hand, many people can be very uncomfortable plainly making their intentions known, even though they have no intention of taking a requested action.

There may be many reasons why this is so. These include fear of losing a friendship or offending someone; not wanting to be perceived as the "bad guy;" wanting to delay a negative or extreme reaction; or any number of reasons.

To have been blessed to have reached advanced age (old as defined by the individual) brings the privilege of not even having to respond. Such a one has only to look at the requesters as if they are crazy for even

Chapter One —OVERVIEW ...

asking, and walk away, ignoring any request with a tacit "No."

There are some key words or phrases that can be a great indicator that the answer is "No." These include, but are not limited to, the following, whether with or without the "Yes," "But only," "Okay," or some other word in the equation.

> Yes, when . . . .
>
> Yes, if . . . .
>
> Yes, but. . . .
>
> Yes, as soon as . . . .

Feel free to use any of these responses that may fit your circumstances from time to time.

Yes, when . . .

Yes, but . . .

Yes, if . . .

Yes, as soon as . . .

CHAPTER TWO

IF...

IF . . .

If I have enough left over.

If you can get me the answers I need first.

If you will watch Bébé's kids (aka BayBay's) for me this weekend.

If I can see my way clear.

If I remember.

If it doesn't rain somewhere.

If I feel better.

If my plane is not delayed.

If my horoscope says it's okay.

If my check gets here in time.

If there's anything left after I pay my bills.

If my car will make it.

Chapter Two — IF ...

If you have insurance (and you know they don't).

Yes, if I can find my keys in time.

Yes, if I can get my _____ to agree (husband, wife, family, mentor, etc).

Yes, if the Committee votes unanimously in favor.

Yes, if the quarantine is lifted by then.

If my cold sore is gone by then.

If you sign your _____ (vehicle, house, etc.) over to me as collateral.

If my doctor says I can.

If my dog (cat, hamster, etc.) likes you.

If you do it first, then maybe.

If my cold sore is gone by then.

If my horoscope says it's okay.

CHAPTER THREE

AS SOON AS...

Yes, AS SOON AS...

Yes, as soon as I lose this extra weight.

Yes, as soon as my _____ moves out.
(Fill in the blank: brother-in-law, mother-in-law, cousin, etc.)

As soon as I get my promotion.

Yes, as soon as I receive the check you said was in the mail.

Chapter Three —AS SOON AS ...

Yes, as soon as my divorce is final.

Yes, as soon as I can save enough money.

Yes, as soon as I can get a handle on things.

Yes, as soon as I get a better job.

Yes, as soon as I win the lotto.

Yes, as soon as I can work it into my budget.

CHAPTER FOUR

WHEN...

WHEN . . .

Yes, when my ship comes in.

Yes, when pigs fly.

When Hell freezes over.

When I find it.

When molasses flows uphill on a cold day.

When I can find the time.

When I die and go to Heaven.

Chapter Four — WHEN ...

When you promise me you'll

_____.

(Fill in the blank)

When you stop being _____.
(crazy, selfish, ignorant, stupid, ugly, dumb, moronic, insane, etc.)

When I get my tax refund check.

When you receive your PhD.

When the chickens come home to roost.

CHAPTER FIVE

BUT...

BUT . . .

Okay, but make sure you have a Plan B.

Okay, but don't hold me to it.

Okay, but don't hold your breath.

Okay, but first you have to pay me back for the last loan.

Okay, but if it doesn't work out, I may not be able to.

Chapter Five — BUT ...

Okay, but first you have to

_____

_____

_____.

(Fill in the blank)

Okay, but only if you

_____

_____

_____.

(Fill in the blank)

CHAPTER SIX

AUTHOR'S PERSPECTIVE AND EXPERIENCES

I believe that, with a few exceptions, it is never really necessary to be brutal with one's honesty, especially if that honesty is unnecessarily hurtful. You don't have to lie; there are acceptable ways around it.

For example, to a mother, there is no such thing as an ugly baby. Truth be told, we know it happens. That being said, here are example responses I have given in kindness when presented with a situation that could be hurtful if I am brutally honest with my opinions. Remember—opinions are not necessarily facts, just beliefs!

"Look at our precious baby. Isn't she beautiful?"

"Oh, just look at her--she is precious!"
"Oh, my goodness! He is going to be a handsome devil!"
"Just look at those plump, rosy cheeks!"
"Oh, my, what a pretty little pink ribbon in her hair. It perfectly matches her adorable pink dress!"

Chapter Six — AUTHOR'S PERSPECTIVE AND EXPERIENCES ...

I would imagine that many a broken relationship, marriage, or friendship may have been saved if hurtful, brutal honesty had not been in play. However, sometimes brute honesty is necessary, depending on the situation as well as the relationship. Following are examples.

"I like this dress. Do you think it looks good on me? Should I buy it?"

"It is a nice dress. If you like how it looks and feels, I'm all for it."

"It is a really nice color, but I think you may find something you might like better if you look a little more."

"I don't want to hurt your feelings, but as your true friend, I can't approve of your buying that dress."

"Do these shoes make my feet look too big?"

"Girl, who's going to be looking at your feet with that neckline!"

"Hey, Sis. Tell me the truth. Why do you think girls always turn me down when I asked them to dance?"

"Brother, you know I love you, so I must tell you the truth. You have to improve your hygiene."

POSSIBLE NEGATIVE RESULT FOR NOT SAYING **NO**

Are there negative consequences when you agree to something when your gut tells you to say "no?" There certainly may be. Let me share an experience I endured years ago when I was single. I have always been a champion of the underdog and often went out of my way to help alleviate hurt I witnessed.

I had gone to a party with my younger sister and her girlfriend. There was nice music, there was dancing, and plenty of single men and women as well as some couples. I noticed one young man in particular that I categorized as an underdog. I watched as he systematically went around the room inviting young ladies to dance with disturbing results. He was

Chapter Six — AUTHOR'S PERSPECTIVE AND EXPERIENCES ...

being brutally and hurtfully rejected by every single person he approached. I felt pained for him as he made his way closer to me. I made the decision that I would not reject him, despite his repulsiveness. Dutifully, I accepted his offer to dance, which I sorely regretted the rest of the night! I don't know what his impression of me was, but I started it and felt obligated to see it through.

My sense of old-fashioned etiquette taught me two things that always resonated with me. In social settings such as dances and parties:

1. The first and the last dance is to be with your escort, and

2. If you refuse an offer to dance with someone, anyone else who asks you to dance for the duration of that song is to be refused as well.

As a result of my "act of kindness," I was stuck with him for the rest of the night. (Rather, he stuck like glue to me, continually asking me to dance. I had performed my one duty, that first dance!) Finally, I was able to signal to my sister that it was time to go!

KINDNESS AND A SMILE CAN SAVE A LIFE

It is better, I am convinced, to lean toward kindness and the high road in life. I am reminded of an incident that happened to my mother years before I was born, the story of which had been repeated throughout the years.

My parents were living in Memphis, Tennessee, where my oldest sister was born. My mother had stepped outside the door and looked up to see this strange man looking menacingly at her. When he started to approach her, she smiled at him, a simple smile. The man stopped in his tracks and said, "Lady, thank God you smiled. I saw your teeth were white and not gold. I was about to kill you."

A PERSONAL EXPERIENCE OF SAYING **NO** WITHOUT SAYING **NO**

When I was 13, I went with a family in my church and their 15-year-old daughter to a Sunday School Convention in Louisville, Kentucky. We left early so the father could visit with relatives in Texarkana, Arkansas, who also had a teen daughter. One night

Chapter Six — AUTHOR'S PERSPECTIVE AND EXPERIENCES ...

the three of us went to a local teen hangout where there was dancing. After a couple of hours of fun, we were preparing to leave.

A young man with whom I had been dancing asked if he could walk me home. I didn't say yes or no. I merely said, "It's a long walk to Los Angeles!"
Eleanor (C-PASS) Jones

CHAPTER SEVEN

RESPONSES YOU HAVE GIVEN

CHAPTER 7

gives you an opportunity to record answers you have given when you definitely did not want to say "Yes" even though the answer was definitely "No."

_____

_____

_____

_____

_____

_____

Chapter Seven — RESPONSES YOU HAVE GIVEN ...

CHAPTER EIGHT

RESPONSES YOU HAVE RECEIVED

CHAPTER 8 gives you an opportunity to record answers you have been given by others who did not actually say "No." These can be helpful as resources for your own use in the future.

_____

_____

_____

_____

_____

_____

_____

Chapter Seven — RESPONSES YOU HAVE RECIEVED ...

How to Say NO Without Saying NO

A LITTLE HELP FROM MY FRIENDS

I invited friends and colleagues to offer input for HOW
TO SAY "NO"
WITHOUT SAYING "NO."

They were asked to provide situations in which
1)   <u>they</u> were asked to do something they really didn't want to do but were reluctant to give a direct answer of no, and

2)   <u>they</u> asked something of someone who really didn't want to do but were reluctant to give a direct answer of no.

Here are the results.

"I was working with an author on her first nonfiction book. She had her mind set on how the interior of the book should be constructed. After thorough examination of the entire project, I conceded to her ideas that were not in conflict with my brand. Instead of saying no to her ideas that were in conflict, I offered samples of what I would do in keeping the integrity of my brand. The book is beautiful.

"Many times during my marriage, I would ask my husband to attend business occasions with me. Rather than giving me a direct answer of "no," he would always respond, 'I can't do that.' "
—Willa Robinson

"At a gathering at my mom's house, everyone wanted something to eat. I only wanted to buy food for my kids and my mom. Someone else wanted something to eat but wanted me to pay for it. I told her I only had enough money for my kids.

"When friends or acquaintances ask for favors, usually involving money, my 'go to' response is, "'I have to pay a bill.'" —**KAL**

"As an instructor in ASL (American Sign Language), I use my skill to my advantage. If it is a stranger, I say nothing but start signing. They usually walk away, assuming I am mute and hearing impaired. So far, I haven't run into anyone who could read sign language!" —**C. Moore**

I have a friend who is always begging for whatever I am eating. It's not that she doesn't have food or the means to get it. She always has an excuse ("I'm not really hungry, I had a late breakfast. But yours looks so good, I just want a little taste.") It's not that I don't like to share. That repetitive scene just got to be too much. One day early last March before the big pandemic shutdown, she went into her ploy. I simply said, "Be my guest, but it's at your own risk. I have been exposed to the virus!"
—**Anonymous**

ABOUT THE AUTHOR

Eleanor is a speaker, Amazon #1 best-selling author, and singer-songwriter. Her stage name and brand is Eleanor "C-PASS" Jones.

Her explosion of creativity has encompassed the knowledge gleaned from her varied background in education, law, finance, music, and life. Besides her fictional publications (the LIV series, Volumes I – III), How to Say 'No' … is her first nonfiction book. Also in progress is a children's book series she is co-authoring with a long-time friend.

She is performing, writing, and marketing her books while returning to public speaking with a target audience of abused and battered women.

Married with children and grands, Eleanor resides in Los Angeles.

www.ingramcontent.com/pod-product-compliance
Lightning Source LLC
Chambersburg PA
CBHW062036120526
44592CB00036B/2197